TINA KENNIMER

Dachshund Delights - A Complete Guide To Your Favorite Wiener Dog

Understanding Their Unique Personality & Charm

In loving memory of Laci, my dear Dachshund companion, who filled my days with joy and warmth. Your playful spirit and unwavering loyalty left paw prints on my heart that will never fade. Though you are gone, your love remains a cherished part of my life. Thank you for the laughter and the cuddles—forever my little sunshine.

Contents

Introduction

The dachshund, affectionately known as the "wiener dog," boasts a captivating history that stretches back to 15th-century Germany. Bred for their remarkable hunting skills, these small but spirited dogs were initially designed to pursue badgers, rabbits, and foxes. By the 1800s, their prowess and loyalty endeared them to many, leading to their rise in popularity. The establishment of the first breed standard in Germany in 1879 marked a pivotal moment for the Dachshund, further solidifying its status as a distinguished breed. As military personnel and immigrants introduced the Dachshund to America, its charm quickly captured hearts, especially after the World Wars. Recognized by the American Kennel Club in 1885, Dachshunds have since become beloved family companions, celebrated for their distinctive looks and vibrant personalities. This book explores the rich legacy of the Dachshund, highlighting its evolution from a skilled hunter to a cherished family member.

This book gives readers a historical overview of the origins and evolution of the Dachshund breed to help readers understand the breed's unique traits and behaviors, therefore fostering a deeper understanding and appreciation for the Dachshund. It is a guide to help potential owners make informed decisions based on breed variations, individual temperaments, and personal circumstances when selecting the right Dachshund. It will also provide information on the specific requirements for Dachshunds, ensuring their physical well-being and longevity, as well as practical training tips to help prevent common behavioral issues and promote positive interactions, enhancing exercise needs in fun, stimulating play to contribute to a happy, healthy, and well-rounded ownership experience.

A brief background about myself: I have had dachshunds for 26 years. I dreamed of having a dachshund throughout my childhood, and in 1996, that dream finally came true. One evening in 1996, the classic movie "The Ugly Dachshund" came on television. At this time, I was going through one of the darkest times in my life. As I watched the movie, I thought, "I have to get myself one of these dogs." Not long after this, I got my first Dachshund. Her name was Laci. She was solid red with tons of wrinkles. We had a fantastic bond, one I have never had with a human. She was my everything. I took her everywhere with me. Laci was very independent, intelligent, rebellious, loving, and funny. When Laci was young, she loved playing fetch with her rope toy. She would bring the toy over and lay it at my feet. That meant she wanted to play. Laci was so human-like, understanding everything I would say to her, probably because I talked to her like a human. She never destroyed anything in the house; she was easy to housebreak and an absolute breeze and delight. She always knew what time it was and when it was the weekend. Once dressed on Sunday mornings, I would go down the street to get a newspaper. Laci would always sit at the front door waiting to ride with me. Laci was always by my side while in nursing school, staying up all night studying for a test with her head lying on my leg. When I had two surgeries, she was right there, making sure I was okay, never leaving my side. I miss her every day. She lived to be 17 years and 10 months old. Before Laci passed, her kidneys started to fail. I did everything I could for her to preserve her life, but

2

one night, after a long, painful night, she let me know it was time. I called and made cremation arrangements for her, and it was the second most challenging thing in my life I had to do. I held her in my arms, wrapped in her blanket, until she took her last breath. Laci gave me so much – her unconditional love and support. The hurt of losing her was engulfing, but the joy and love of having her around for almost 18 years was well worth it.

Today, I have three dachshunds, all short-haired. Isabella 14, Maddie 6, and Holly 4. I cannot imagine my life without a Dachshund in it. They keep me on my toes and in stitches with the funny things they do. Complete bliss!!

That said, it is essential to understand Dachshund's personality. These small dogs are independent, curious, intelligent, funny, determined, stubborn, fearless, strong, fast, sweet, and loyal. They are interested in everything! Nothing, absolutely nothing gets by a Dachshund. A Dachshund always wants to be with you, and they have a sense of ownership over you and your home. You are servant to your Dachshund. Be prepared. There is no sound, a peep, or a squash of a bug that gets by your Dachshund. If someone approaches 100 feet away, they know and will alert you. If you try to outsmart your dog, remember it will not work. All you can do is be patient and love them.

Despite their long bodies, they are swift and agile. They love to dig, which is what they were born to do, and if you have moles, they are great mole catchers. They also love to chase squirrels. Their nose is always to the ground, attempting to forage for a snack or run down the scent of another animal. On the flip side, they love to lounge on the couch, burrow in blankets, and snuggle up close to you. They love attention, and they love the scent of their owner. Dachshunds are the best, but they are not for everyone. Ensure the breed you choose is correct for you and your family.

Chapter 1: The Dachshund Breed

Origin and History of Dachshunds

The dachshund, affectionately known as the "wiener dog," has a long rich history that dates back several centuries. The breed originated in Germany, with ties going back as far as the 15th century. Dachshund

comes from the German words "Dachs" (badger) and 'Hund" (dog) and
were bred for hunting purposes to hunt small game such as badgers,
rabbits, and foxes. The breed gained significant popularity by the
1800s for its hunting abilities and loyal companionship. In 1879,
the first official breed standard was established in Germany. The
smooth-haired Dachshund was the first original Dachshund; the first
wire-haired Dachshund came onto the scene in 1812, and the long-
haired Dachshund debuted in 1820. Those in the military, immigrants
to America, and those wealthy enough to travel abroad brought the
Dachshund breed to the United States in the late 19th century. After
World War I and II, it became a beloved household pet in various media
and popular culture forms. In 1885, the American Kennel Club (AKC)
officially recognized the breed, and today is one of the most popular
dog breeds in the U.S. Dachshunds are cherished family pets, known for
their distinct appearance and lively personalities. Their unique traits
and enduring charm have made them a favorite among dog enthusiasts
worldwide.

Popularity and Cultural Significance

Dachshunds' popularity grew in Germany, leading to many local clubs.
In 1895, breeders began breeding and producing for the show ring,
increasing the size and depth of the chest. The Dachshund became the
most popular dog shown in the ring in 1895. The Miniature Dachshund
Club was formed in 1905. In 1909 independent clubs came together
and formed one club known as the Association of German Working
Dachshund Clubs, which helped to unify breeders working together
until World War I. Dachshunds have remained around for centuries
due to the dedication of breeders and owners who have successfully
made the Dachshund what it is today.

Different Types: Short-haired, Long-haired, and Wire-haired

There are three types of Dachshunds: Short-haired, long-haired, and wired-haired (a mix between dachshund and schnauzer).

Short-haired Dachshunds

The short-haired should be short, smooth, and shiny. The hair should
not be too long or thick, fine or thin, or have bald patches. The ears
should not be leathery, and the tail should be covered with hair and
come to a gradual point. A hairless or brush tail is a fault.

Wire-haired Dachshunds

The wire-haired should be uniformly covered with a dense, wiry coat and thin, short-hair undercoat. The absence of an undercoat is a fault. The facial features include bushy eyebrows and beard. The hair on the ears is shorter than that on the body and may appear smooth. Any soft hair in the outer coat, especially on top of the head, short hair without a beard and eyebrows is also considered a fault. Any long, wavy, or curly hair is also a fault. The tail should come to a gradual point with coarse close-fitting hair without a brush.

Long-haired Dachshunds

The long-haired Dachshunds have long, silky, sometime wavy hair. The hair is longer under the neck, on the ears, and back of the legs where it feathers. The hair on the ears should always extend beyond the lower edge of the ears. Curly hair, short hair on the ears, a pronounced parting on the back, or long hair between the toes is a fault.

Size Variations and Breed Standards

There are also two sizes: Standard and miniature. In the U.S., standard Dachshunds are considered to be between 16 and 32 pounds while miniature Dachshunds are less than 11 pounds at age 1 year.

Chapter 2: Unique Personality Traits

Overview of Dachshund Temperament

Dachshunds are known for their unique personalities and charming temperaments.Potential owners should understand their temperament and know what to expect before bringing a Dachshund home.

Common Personality Traits

- **Lively and Energetic:** Dachshunds are playful and spirited. They love toys and enjoy regular playtime and exercise.
- **Courageous and Bold:** Dachshunds are often fearless. They are known as "big dogs in small bodies". Being bred for hunting, they can be tenacious.
- **Loyal and Affectionate:** Dachshunds are known to be extremely loving and form strong bonds with their owners. They look at their owner as part of their pack.
- **Stubbornness:** Dachshunds are independent and often exhibit stubborn behavior, which can pose a challenge when in training. However, with consistency and positive reinforcement, training

can be accomplished.

- **Curious and Intelligent:** Dachshunds tend to be inquisitive and love to explore their surroundings. Mental stimulation is essential, and dog brain games are a fun way to incorporate cognitive stimulation.
- **Protective:** Dachshunds are protective of their property and owners.They make excellent watchdogs and are wary of strangers. Only approach a Dachshund with permission from the owner.
- **Socialization Needs:** Early socialization is crucial to help them develop good manners and reduce any potential for aggression or shyness around other pets and people.

Dachshunds are loving, playful, and sometimes a bit quirky, making them delightful companions!

How Personality Affects Behavior and Training

Dachshund's personality traits can significantly influence their behavior and training but can quickly be achieved with patience and consistency.

- **Stubbornness:** Dachshunds have an independent streak, making them resistant to commands. Consistent, patient training with positive reinforcement is essential. Using treats specifically for training and praise will help to motivate your Dachshund.
- **Intelligence and Curiosity:** Dachshunds are smart and inquisitive. Engaging them with puzzle toys or training sessions will help keep them entertained and prevent boredom-related bad behavior.
- **Affectionate Nature:** Dachshunds' strong bond with their owner means they respond well to love and praise. Building a trusting relationship with your Dachshund can inhibit their willingness to

learn and follow commands.

- **Boldness:** Dachshunds are fearless, tend to take risks, and challenge their boundaries. Establishing boundaries and rules early can help manage their behavior effectively.
- **Socialization Needs:** Early exposure to various environments, people, and other pets is crucial. A well-socialized Dachshund tends to be more confident and less prone to anxiety or aggression.
- **Protective Instincts:** Dachshunds are excellent watchdogs but can exhibit excessive or unnecessary barking. Proper training can control this behavior.
- **Playfulness:** Dachshunds need playtime and regular exercise. Making training fun for your Dachshund helps to keep them engaged and makes learning enjoyable for them.

Understanding these personality traits allows for more effective training techniques and helps to create a positive environment for both the Dachshund and their owner.

Chapter 3: Health and Care

Common Health Issues in Dachshunds

I feel compelled to tell you about one of Dachshund's most common health concerns. Overall, Dachshunds are healthy dogs, but there is one downfall. Well, it's not an actual downfall, but you must research so if it does happen, you are prepared and know where the closest vet emergency room is. Because Dachshunds have such long bodies, they are at risk for Intervertebral Disc Disease (IVDD). IVDD is a neurological disorder that happens when the intervertebral disc becomes diseased or compresses the spinal cord which can lead to pain, weakness, and even paralysis. To help prevent IVDD, Dachshunds must avoid jumping on anything; couch, chair, bed, you name it. Now, if your Dachshund is like mine, Isabella's IVDD injury happened while she was outside chasing a squirrel and there was no way I could have prevented it. She chased a squirrel up one of our cedar porch posts and twisted her back when she jumped up. Three days later, she lost the use of her back legs. I rushed her to the ER, where we then took her to have emergency surgery. She recovered without any complications and has never had any more back issues. The one thing I would suggest if you are getting a Dachshund is a ramp. The one I use for my three Dachshunds, which I highly recommend is from **www.alphapaw.com.** I paid $125 for mine,

the best $125 I have ever spent. They think it is a toy. You may think
this is expensive, but it is pennies in the bucket compared to $15,000
to have back surgery. And yes, that is about what it cost today for the
surgery, as we were faced with this again with another one of our dogs
in June 2024, which thank goodness, we did not have to go through
with it.

Another common concern I feel compelled to talk about is obesity
in your Dachshund. Dachshunds are just like people. When you
carry around excess weight, it is hard on your joints. Obesity is hard
on a Dachshund's joints and back, which can contribute to IVDD.
Dachshunds are already very low to the ground. If they have excess
weight, it can lead to their chest or bellies dragging the ground and
causing more health issues. I highly recommend monitoring your
Dachshund's weight throughout the year and adjusting their nutrition
accordingly. I recommend speaking to your veterinarian to devise a
plan for your Dachshund's health and longevity.

Nutrition and Dietary Needs

Dachshunds are notorious for inhaling their food, which can cause
them to choke, so I recommend giving them small pieces. They are also
little food disposals. They will eat until they are sick. During feeding
times, monitoring the amount of food your Dachshund eats is a good
idea, especially if you have more than one pet, and never give your
Dachshund table food. Giving table food can lead to obesity, not to
mention that many human foods and spices are toxic to animals. Talk
to your veterinarian regarding which food is best for you and your
Dachshund. There are many commercial brands, but my favorite is
something that is more natural and healthier, like freeze-dried food. Be

sure to put your Dachshund on a feeding schedule. Puppies will need to eat more often, while older Dachshunds usually will eat twice a day; morning and evening are sufficient, but depending on your situation, it may differ. Dachshunds are routine-oriented, so they expect to eat simultaneously every day.

Regular Vet Check-ups and Preventive Care

It is always a good idea to take your Dachshund to the veterinarian for a check-up within two weeks of bringing it home, sooner if possible. There are essential preventative measures to keep your little bundle of joy healthy. You should worm puppies at 4 weeks, 6 weeks, 8 weeks, 6 months, and 9 months.

After that your veterinarian will worm your pet upon getting its vaccinations. Depending on your dog's lifestyle and geographical location, vaccinations for puppies would be on the following vaccination schedule:

- 8 weeks: DHPP (distemper, hepatitis, parainfluenza, parvovirus), Bordetella
- 12 weeks: DHPP, Leptospirosis, canine influenza, Lyme disease
- 16 weeks: DHPP, Leptospirosis, Rabies, boosters for canine influenza, Lyme disease
- Annual checkups: Rabies (every 3 years), DHPP (every 3 years), Leptospirosis (annually)

It is essential that your pet be vaccinated and should be vaccinated on a regular schedule to help maintain immunity and protect your pet form severe illness.

Grooming Tips for Different Coat Types

Short-haired Coat

Short-haired coats are the easiest to groom. Most Dachshunds typically do not like grooming and will run from you, but others enjoy it. Short-haired coats require less grooming than the other type of coats. Dachshund coats are sometimes repellent to water, so try to wet their coat down the best you can. Add shampoo to their hair, and gently lather your dog with your hand or a mitt. They love it when you massage their backs, and stroking your dog's coat helps to get rid of loose hairs. Rinse your dog well, avoid getting water in their ears, and towel dry. Easy!

Long-haired Coat

You can choose to groom your long-haired Dachshund at home or use a trustworthy professional groomer. If you choose to groom at home, you may want to have the following equipment: a fine to medium toothed comb, a pin brush, tangle remover, and blunt edge scissors. The long-haired coats need more frequent and aggressive grooming than the short-haired coats, approximately twice a week. Be sure to check for twigs and leaves before starting the grooming process. Comb or brush long-haired coats daily with a pin brush to prevent tangles and matting. You want to brush or comb your long-haired in the natural direction of the hair. There are detangling products on the market that you can use that are specific to dogs. Before brushing, allow your dog to lie on a flat surface, and run your fingers through their hair to loosen any tangles, allowing for easier brushing and less discomfort for your dog.

Using the blunt-edged scissors, you need to trim around their feet and between their toes. Because Dachshunds do not like their feet handled, you will need to have someone to help you keep them still. You will also need someone to keep them still while you trim under their tail. Hold the tail out straight from the base, trim the underside to prevent the dog from soiling itself during defecation. Using the same blunt-edged scissors, you want to cut any fine hair around the genital area as well as around the rectum.

Wired-haired Coat

For the wired-hair coat you may need the following equipment: a hound glove or mitt, a stripping comb, a medium-toothed comb, a pin brush, blunt-edged scissors, and thinning scissors. A rough or tight coated wire is similar to short-haired and requires little care, usually a weekly brushing. Always check for twigs or burs that may get tangled in the hair before grooming. Use the stripping scissors to thin out guard hairs. Use it gently down the back on a slant, just skimming on an angle. You never want to dig into the coat. For the beard and eyebrows, you can run a comb through them as often as needed to keep them from tangling. If they get too long or thick, you can use the thinning scissors to help thin them out. Never pull the dog's hair when pulling away from the beard; use short, quick motions. Just like the long-haired coat, you want to trim around the genitals and rectum to avoid tangling.

19

Nails

Check your Dachshund's nails regularly to make sure they do not become too long. Long nails can start to curl under and grow into the skin, causing pain and changes in the posture of the paw impairing the dog's ability to walk. Black nails are more difficult to trim as you are unable to view the quick – the portion through which blood flows. You can trim your dog's nails with dog nail clippers or a Dremel, or you may choose to let a professional groomer, or your veterinarian trim them. Either way, regular nail trims are a vital part of keeping your Dachshund healthy and happy.

Chapter 4: Training Your Dachshund

Importance of Early Socialization and Training

Early socialization and training are crucial for a Dachshund for several reasons:

- **Behavioral Development:** Early socialization helps Dachshunds become well-adjusted adults. It exposes them to various environments, people, and other animals, reducing the likelihood of fear or aggression later in life.
- **Preventing Behavioral Issues:** Dachshunds can develop anxiety and stubbornness if not properly socialized. Early training helps prevent common issues like excessive barking, digging, or aggression.
- **Building Confidence:** Socialization helps build a Dachshund's confidence, making them more adaptable to new experiences and less prone to fear-based reactions.
- **Strengthening the Bond:** Training sessions create a strong bond between the dog and owner, fostering trust and communication.
- **Mental Stimulation:** Early training provides mental challenges that keep a Dachshund engaged and focused, which is especially important for this intelligent breed.

- **Establishing Good Manners:** Training teaches basic commands and manners, making it easier to integrate them into family life and public situations.
- **Reducing Health Risks:** A well-socialized dog is less likely to experience stress-related health issues, which can arise from fear or anxiety.

Early socialization and training set the foundation for a happy, healthy, and well-behaved dachshund.

Effective Training Techniques and Tips

Training a Dachshund can be a rewarding experience, as they are intelligent and eager to please, though they can also be stubborn. Here are some effective training techniques and tips specifically for Dachshunds:

- **Positive Reinforcement:** Use high quality treats, and playtime as rewards for good behavior. Always reward your dog immediately after the desired behavior so they make a distinct connection.
- **Consistency is Key:** Using the same commands and cues consistently will help them understand your expectations.
- **Short Training Sessions:** To help maintain their attention, keep training sessions short, about 5-10 minutes, and repeat them throughout the day.
- **Socialization:** Early on, take your dog on outings to introduce it to different environments, people and other pets, as this helps to reduce fear, anxiety, and aggression later.
- **Focus on Basic Commands:** Start with basic commands like "sit," "stay," "come," and "down." With these simple commands on board,

you can introduce more complex commands.

- **Use Leash Training:** Start leash training early to prevent pulling or chasing. Use a vest harness, if necessary, as Dachshunds can be prone to back injuries.

- **Address Behavioral Issues Early:** If your Dachshund shows signs of aggression or anxiety, address these behaviors promptly. If needed, consider consulting with a behavioral specialist or a professional trainer.
- **Patience and Persistence:** Be patient; Dachshunds can take time

to learn. Remain calm and be persistent, even if they don't respond immediately.

- **Engage Their Senses**: Use toys and puzzle to stimulate their minds. Incorporate scent work or games that encourage them to use their noses.
- **Make it Fun:** Keep training fun and engaging. Integrate games and play into training sessions and leave the sessions on a positive note to keep them eager for the next round.
- **Avoid Negative Reinforcement:** Never use physical punishment or harsh corrections; it can damage the bond and trust between you and your dog. Concentrate instead on redirecting unwanted behaviors positively.
- **Regular Exercise:** Make certain your Dachshund gets regular exercise. Physical activity helps reduce hyperactivity and improves focus during training.

You can effectively train your Dachshund using these techniques and tips while building a strong, positive relationship!

Addressing Common Behavioral Issues

Dachshunds, like all breeds, can develop behavioral issues. Here are some common problems and strategies for addressing them:

- **Barking:** Dachshunds are known for their alertness, which can lead to excessive barking. Identify the triggers and desensitize your dog gradually. You may use commands like "quiet" and reward them when they stop barking.
- **Separation Anxiety:** Dachshunds can become attached and may struggle when left alone. Starting with short periods of alone time,

increasing the length of time gradually can acclimate them to being alone. Provide toys and puzzles to keep them occupied. Consider using calming aids or techniques, such as leaving a piece of your clothing with them. Having your scent close by gives them a sense of security.

- **Potty Training Issues:** Dachshunds can be very stubborn about potty training. Some may take longer than others. Be patient! Bathroom breaks need to be consistent, and positive reinforcement should always be used immediately after they go outside. Consider crate training, as dogs usually avoid soiling their sleeping area.

- **Pulling on Leash:** Dachshunds may pull due to excitement or curiosity. Use a harness instead of a collar with a Dachshund. Dachshunds are notorious for inching out of a collar and can sometimes inch out of a vest harness. Practice loose-leash walking by stopping when they pull and rewarding them when they stay beside you. Use high-value treats that are different from their everyday at home treats.

- **Aggression or Fearfulness:** This may stem from lack of socialization or negative experiences. Gradually introduce them to new people, animals, and environments in a controlled manner. Use positive reinforcement to reward calm behavior. If aggression persists, consider seeking help from a behavioral specialist or professional trainer.

- **Digging:** Dachshunds may dig out of boredom or to explore. Increase physical and mental stimulation through exercise and interactive toys. Dachshunds are natural-born diggers, so you may want to provide a designated digging area and encourage them to use that space.

- **Destructive Chewing:** In younger dogs, chewing occurs due to boredom, anxiety, or teething. Provide plenty of chew toys and alternate them to maintain your dog's interest. Supervise them when they're not in their crate and redirect them to appropriate items. Ensuring they get enough exercise to reduce excess energy can cut down on some of the destructive behavior.

- **Jumping Up:** Dogs jump up due to excitement or to seek attention. Teach an alternative behavior, like sitting, when greeting people. Ignore them when they jump and only give attention when they are calm.
- **Food Aggression:** Arises from resource-guarding instincts. Avoid feeding them near other pets, and gradually desensitize them to your presence during mealtime, and feed treats to build trust and reduce aggression.
- **Picky Eating:** Dachshunds can be particular about their food. Maintain a consistent feeding schedule and avoid giving too many treats. If you need to change your pet's food, use a graduated amount in the transition phase to prevent stomach upset.

You can help your Dachshund become a well-adjusted and happy companion by addressing these issues with patience and consistency!

Fun Activities and Games That Cater to Their Personality

Dachshunds are playful, curious, and energetic, making them great companions for fun activities and games. Here are some ideas that cater to their unique personality:

- **Scent Games:** A hound dog will always use their nose. Hide treats around the house or yard and encourage your Dachshund to find them using their nose. Creating trails with treats for them to follow is fun for them. Start easy and gradually increase the difficulty.
- **Interactive Toys and Puzzles:** Invest in puzzle toys that require your Dachshund to solve problems to access treats. According to dog behavior experts, this stimulates their mind and keeps them engaged.
- **Agility Training:** Set up a mini agility course with tunnels, jumps, and weave poles. Dachshunds love to run and explore, and this is a fantastic way to exercise their body and mind. It also strengthens the bond between dog and owner, and it is fun for both.
- **Fetch:** Use a soft ball or toy that's easy for them to carry. Due to their body shape, they may not fetch like other breeds, but many Dachshunds enjoy chasing and retrieving.
- **Tug-of-War:** Play a gentle game of tug-of-war with a sturdy rope toy, as it can help with bonding and provide a good workout, but ensure you teach them to release on command.
- **Obstacle Courses:** Use cushions, chairs, and other household items to create a fund obstacle course. Encourage your Dachshund to navigate through it for treats.

- **Doggy Playdates:** Arrange playdates with other dogs to allow for socialization. Supervised play with well-matched playmates can be very stimulating.
- **Training Sessions with Tricks:** Teach them fun tricks like rolling over, playing dead, or shaking paws. Use positive reinforcement to keep it fun and engaging.
- **Swimming:** If your Dachshund enjoys water, take them for a swim in a safe environment. Always supervise them closely, as not all Dachshunds are natural swimmers. I recommend using a life jacket to keep your little swimmer safe.
- **Long Walks or Hikes:** Take your Dachshund on walks or hikes in nature. They love nature walks; exploring new scents and sights

can be enriching.

- **Bubble Chasing:** Blow dog-safe bubbles for them to chase and pop. Many dogs find this activity incredibly entertaining!
- **Hide and Seek with You:** Find a spot in your home and call your Dachshund to find you. This game helps reinforce their recall skills.
- **Kong or Treat-Dispensing Toys:** Fill Kong with peanut butter or other tasty fillings and freeze it. This will keep them occupied and mentally stimulated.
- **Dog Sports:** Investigate dog sports like scent work or lure coursing, which taps into dogs' hunting instincts. These can be a fun way to exercise and engage with their instincts.
- **Seasonal Activities:** In the winter, they may enjoy playing in the snow, while in summer, they might love to explore a dog-friendly beach. Always provide appropriate gear to keep them safe.

These activities provide physical exercise and stimulate your Dachshund mentally, keeping them happy and healthy!

Chapter 5: Building A Strong Bond

Understanding Your Dachshund's Need for Companionship

Understanding your Dachshund's need for companionship is critical to ensuring their well-being and happiness. Dachshunds are pack animals by nature, stemming from their origins as hunting dogs, and are only comfortable within a pack. They thrive on social interaction and tend to bond closely with their families. They love to spend quality time with their owner, whether it is on the couch, playing games, or going for walks. It does not matter about the quantity of time you spend with them but the quality. Your presence is crucial for their well-being. Giving them attention and affection when you are together is what they crave. If you must leave home for work or other essentials, provide them something that carries your scent, like a toy, blanket, or piece of clothing. If you are frequently away from home, consider adding another pet. A companion can help alleviate loneliness when you're not around. Whenever possible, take your Dachshund with you on outings. Many stores welcome dogs, meaning you can bring your furry friend along to enhance their social experiences and strengthen the bond between you and your Dachshund while providing an enjoyable car ride. By understanding and catering to your Dachshund's need for companionship, you can create a loving and secure environment that fosters their happiness and well-being.

The Role of Positive Enforcement in Bonding

Positive reinforcement helps with immediate training and contributes to long-term behavior stability. A well-behaved Dachshund is likely to be happier and more secure in its relationship with you. By incorporating positive reinforcement into your training and interactions, you foster a strong, trusting bond with your Dachshund, enhancing its overall well-being and happiness.

Communicating Effectively with Your Dachshund

Effective communication with your Dachshund is essential for building a solid bond and ensuring a harmonious relationship. Use open and inviting postures, a cheerful, encouraging tone when they do something right, and a calm, firm tone when redirecting unwanted behavior. Your tone conveys your feelings and intentions. To help establish a connection, make eye contact with your Dachshund; it will make them feel more engaged during interactions. If your dog becomes distracted by noise, incorporate verbal commands with hand signals. Recognize when your Dachshund needs space or time to relax, especially if it is highly anxious; it will find a quiet place alone to relax - allowing this time when it feels overwhelmed shows respect for their feelings. By implementing these strategies, you can foster a deeper understanding and connection with your Dachshund, leading to a happier and more fulfilling relationship.

Chapter 6: Living with a Dachshund

Creating a Safe Environment for Your Dachshund

Creating a Dachshund-friendly environment is essential for their well-being and happiness. Designate a comfortable space in your home with a crate, cozy bed, or blanket where your Dachshund can relax and feel secure. Provide easy access to the couch or bed for lounging, but please use a ramp as they must not be jumping up or down as they are prone to back injuries. Some floors can be very slippery for your Dachshund, so using rugs or mats will help prevent injuries. Minimize loud noises and chaotic situations that can stress your Dachshund. You want to create a calm environment, especially during training or relaxation time. Ensure your pet always has access to fresh water in a quiet, accessible area. Ensure that small objects, toxic plants, and chemicals are out of your Dachshunds reach. Dachshunds are curious and may ingest harmful items. If your pet ingests harmful items, contact Pet Poison Control at 888-426-4435. You also want a safe and secure yard fenced properly to prevent escapes. Dachshunds love to dig, so make sure to check the fence line for any escape routes frequently. By creating a Dachshund-friendly environment that prioritizes their safety, comfort, and engagement, you can help your furry friend thrive and feel at home!

Travel Tips and Outings with Your Dachshund

Going on outings and traveling with your Dachshund can be a fun adventure, but it requires some planning to ensure their comfort and safety. To prepare, make sure your pet is current on all vaccinations and ensure the pet's collar has an ID tag that includes your correct information. You may want to consider microchipping your pet. Make sure you use a well-ventilated crate or carrier for traveling and add in their favorite blanket and toy. Pack their essentials: Food, water, and bowls for the trip, and plan to make frequent stops to allow your Dachshund to stretch, relieve themselves, and hydrate. Keep an eye on the temperature, especially in hot weather, and never leave your pet alone in the vehicle. Ensure that the place you will be staying on vacation is pet friendly

prior to leaving home, and that you understand their pet policies. Always have an emergency plan, know where the closest veterinarian clinic is at your destination, and keep a pet first aid kit handy. You can never be too prepared! Most importantly, try to keep the same routine on vacation that you have at home or as close to it as possible. Dachshunds are routine-oriented regarding eating, playing, and spending time with you. By following these tips, you and your Dachshund are sure to have a fun experience making memories together on your outings.

Chapter 7: Celebrating Dachshund Culture

Dachshunds in Popular Media and Pop Culture

Dachshunds have appeared in various art forms, including paintings, sculptures, and even in popular animated shows, often symbolizing loyalty and cuteness. People have also found them in many extraordinaire places. Many famous people have owned Dachshunds: Gary Cooper (Actor), Marlon Brando (Actor), Andy Warhol (Artist), John Wayne (Actor), William Randolph Hearst (Publisher), Napoleon (French Emperor), Josh Duhamel (Singer, Actor), Cole Porter (Composer), E.B. White (Author), and Dita Von Teese (Burlesque Star) just to name a few. Dachshunds are featured in many TV commercials as well as movies including The Secret Life of Pets, The Ugly Dachshund, Weiner Dog Nationals, Bachelor Flat, and Toy Story. And let's not forget about Crusoe the Celebrity Dachshund who has traveled the world, won a People's Choice Award for 2018s "Animal Star," has his own YouTube channel, has written a New York Times bestselling book "Adventures of The Wiener Dog Extraordinaire Crusoe the Celebrity Dachshund." These little guys with their unique looks and spirited personalities continue to capture the hearts of many, making them a beloved breed in various forms of media and pop culture!

Community Events: Dachshund Races and Meet-ups

Dachshund races and meet-ups are fantastic community events celebrating the breed while fostering socialization among dogs and their owners. Dachshund races are held all over the U.S. and are fun competitions where Dachshunds sprint short distances in a roped-off, closed-in area. Winners often receive ribbons, trophies, or fun prizes, adding to the competitive spirit. Some have even gone on winning some big titles. Dachshunds meet-ups are casual gatherings that may occur in dog parks, community centers, or pet-friendly venues where owners socialize, share tips, and let their dogs play together. Many local Dachshund clubs and organizations or breed-specific organizations host regular events, including races and meet-ups, that you may consider joining to stay informed about upcoming events. Participating in Dachshund races and meet-ups is a great way to celebrate your furry friend, meet fellow Dachshund enthusiasts, and build a supportive community!

Books, Websites, and Social Media for Dachshund Lovers

For Dachshund lovers, there are plenty of books, websites, and social media accounts celebrating this adorable breed. Here's an organized list to help you dive deeper into the world of Dachshunds:

Books

"The Dachshund: A Comprehensive Guide" by John R. Bruni: A detailed resource covering breed history, training tips, health care, and more.

"Dachshunds: A Complete Pet Owner's Manual" by Peter J. Pruvost: This manual offers insights into caring for Dachshunds, including training, health, and nutrition.

"The Art of Raising a Dachshund" by Stephanie S. V.: A humorous and informative look at the joys and challenges of Dachshund ownership.

"Dachshund: The Long and Short of It" by Janet Vorwald Dohner: This book covers everything from breed history to grooming and training tips, perfect for new and seasoned owners alike.

"Wiener Dog Art: A Collection of Dachshund Illustrations" by various artists: A delightful collection of artworks celebrating Dachshunds, perfect for decorating your home.

Websites

Dachshund Club of America (DCA): dachshundclubofamerica.org - The official club for Dachshund enthusiasts, offering resources on breed standards, health, and events.

Dachshund Rescue Organizations provide information on adoption, fostering, and volunteering.

Dachshund Life: dachshundlife.com - A website dedicated to all things

Dachshund, featuring articles on care, training, and community events.

The Doxie Blog: A blog focused on dachshund health, training tips, and owner stories, often featuring guest posts from other Dachshund lovers.

Social Media

Instagram: Look for popular accounts like @dachshundworld and @dachshund_daily, which share adorable photos and stories of Dachshunds from around the world. Hashtags: Explore hashtags like #Dachshund, #Doxie, and #WienerDog for a plethora of cute photos and videos.

Facebook Groups: Join groups like Dachshund Lovers and Dachshund Nation where owners share tips, photos, and support each other in their Dachshund journeys.

TikTok: Search for Dachshund-related content by looking up hashtags like #Dachshund or accounts dedicated to Dachshund antics and training.

YouTube: Channels like Dachshund Station and Wiener Dog Central offer entertaining and informative videos about Dachshund care, training, and daily life.

These resources provide information, support, and community for anyone passionate about Dachshunds. Whether you're a new owner or a long-time fan, there's plenty to explore!

The Significance of Breed-Specific Rescues and Advocacy

Breed-specific rescues and advocacy play a crucial role in the welfare of dogs, mainly breeds like Dachshunds. Breed-specific rescues are well-versed in Dachshunds' unique characteristics, health issues, and behavioral traits, enabling them to provide tailored care and support. They often have experience with the breed's specific training and socialization needs, ensuring dogs receive appropriate rehabilitation. Breed-specific rescues help find homes for Dachshunds in need, whether abandoned, surrendered, or coming from shelters, reducing the number of dogs euthanized due to lack of space. They also help facilitate the adoption process, helping potential owners understand what to expect and how to care for their new Dachshund. Many rescues provide necessary medical treatment, including vaccinations, spaying/neutering, and addressing breed-specific health issues (like back problems common in Dachshunds). Rescues often use foster homes, providing a loving environment for dogs before they are adopted, which helps reduce stress and anxiety. Rescues educate the public about the breed, promoting responsible ownership and understanding of Dachshund-specific needs. They advocate for the rights and welfare of Dachshunds, addressing issues like puppy mills, breed discrimination, and health problems associated with poor breeding practices. Breed-specific rescues create a community of Dachshund lovers who can share experiences, resources, and support. They often organize events like meet-ups, races, and fundraisers that raise money and foster community spirit among Dachshund owners. Many rescues promote spaying and neutering to help control the dog population and reduce the number of homeless pets. They emphasize responsible breeding practices to ensure healthier dogs and to prevent overbreeding. Many breed-specific rescues offer

42

support even after adoption, providing resources and advice to help owners navigate challenges. Rescues offer opportunities for community members to get involved through volunteering, fostering, or supporting events, fostering a sense of community and shared purpose. By supporting breed-specific rescues and advocacy groups, Dachshund lovers can significantly impact the lives of these dogs, ensuring they receive the care and love they deserve while promoting responsible ownership and awareness.

Conclusion

Recap of the Joys of Owning a Dachshund

Owning a Dachshund brings a unique set of joys that make them a beloved companion for many. Dachshunds are known for their loving and loyal nature. They often form strong bonds with their owners, providing companionship and emotional support. Their playful and spirited demeanor brings fun and laughter to everyday life. Dachshunds love to play games, chasing toys, and engaging in silly antics that can brighten your day. With their long bodies, short legs, and expressive faces, Dachshunds have an undeniably charming distinctive look. Their appearance often elicits smiles and compliments from others. Dachshunds are intelligent and curious, making them engaging pets. They love to explore their surroundings, and their inquisitive nature keeps life interesting. Their compact size makes them great for various living situations, whether in a small apartment or a large house. They adapt well to different environments. Dachshunds can be wonderful family pets. They often get along well with children and other pets. making them great additions to family life. With consistent training and positive reinforcement, Dachshunds can learn a variety of commands and tricks. Their eagerness to please can make training sessions enjoyable. Owning a dog, including Dachshunds, can promote a healthier lifestyle. Regular walks and playtime encourage physical activity for both you and your pup. Despite their small size, Dachshunds are known for their protective instincts. They often alert their owners to any unusual activity, making them surprisingly good watchdogs. Dachshund ownership usually leads to connections with other Dachshund lovers through local meet-ups, online groups, or community events, fostering a sense of belonging. Dachshunds love to accompany their owners on outings, whether it's a walk in the park, a hike, or a trip to dog-friendly cafes, making every adventure more enjoyable. Owning a Dachshund is a rewarding experience filled with love, laughter, and lifelong companionship. Their unique personality and charm make them truly special pets!

Final Thoughts on the Lifelong Journey With Your Dachshund

Embarking on a lifelong journey with your Dachshund is a rewarding experience filled with love, joy, and unforgettable moments. Dachshunds have a remarkable ability to love deeply and unconditionally. Their affectionate nature will bring warmth to your heart, making every day brighter. From daily walks to weekend getaways, your Dachshund will be your loyal companion through life's adventures. These shared experiences create lasting memories that you'll cherish forever. Owning a Dachshund is an opportunity for continuous learning. You'll discover their unique quirks, needs, and behaviors, deepening your understanding of canine companionship. Caring for your Dachshund encourages a healthier lifestyle. Regular exercise and outdoor activities benefit both of you, fostering a strong bond while keeping you active. Like any relationship, there will be challenges—

training, health issues, or behavioral quirks. Embrace their quirks and celebrate their individuality, as these traits are what make them truly special. Navigating these challenges together fosters resilience and strengthens your bond. Your journey may introduce you to a vibrant community of fellow Dachshund lovers. Sharing experiences, tips, and support enriches your life and enhances your Dachshund's experience. As a Dachshund owner, you can advocate for the breed, promoting responsible ownership and supporting rescue efforts, and help ensure a brighter future for other Dachshunds. The love and joy your Dachshund brings you will leave a lasting impact on your heart. Their playful spirit and unwavering loyalty will enrich your life in countless ways. Finally, cherish every moment—whether it's the quiet snuggles, playful antics, or shared adventures. Each day with your Dachshund is a gift that contributes to a beautiful lifelong journey. Your Dachshund will become more than just a pet; they will be a cherished family member and a lifelong friend, enriching your life in ways you can't imagine. Embrace the journey and enjoy every step along the way!

If you found this book to be helpful, I would be very appreciative if you left a favorable review for the book on Amazon.

Resources and References

Carey, A. (1995). *The dachshund: An owner's guide to a happy healthy pet.* A Simon & Schuster Macmillan Company.

Dachshund Central Team. (n.d.). The fascinating history of the dachshund. *Dachshund Central.* https://dachshund-central.com/the-fascinating-history-of-the-dachshund/

Fiedelmeier, L. (1994). *Dachshunds: A complete pet owner's manual.* Barron's Educational Series, Inc.

Koehler, R. (2024). Essential vaccinations for dogs: From puppies to seniors. *HealthNews.* https://healthnews.com/pet-insurance/pet-care/essential-vaccinations-for-dogs-schedule/

OpenAI. (2024). *ChatGPT (GPT-4)* [Software]. OpenAI. https://www.openai.com/

Packer, R. M. A., Seath, I. J., O'Neill, D. G., Decker, S. D., & Volk, H. A. (2016). DachsLife 2015: An investigation of lifestyle associations with the risk of intervertebral disc disease in dachshunds. *Canine Medicine and Genetics*, 3, Article 5. https://doi.org/10.1186/s40575-016-0039-8

Pet Poison Control. (n.d.). *ASPCA animal poison control.* https://www.aspca.org/pet-care/animal-poison-control

Terry, B. (2021). How to train your dachshund: Basic tips to advanced methods. *Dach World.* https://www.dachworld.com/how-to-train-a-dachshund/

Trupanion Staff. (2024). Meet the miniature dachshund. *Trupanion.* https://www.trupanion.com/pet-blog/article/miniature-dachshund#:~:text=In%20the%20late%201800s%2C%20German%20hunters%20started%20breeding,the%20litter%2C%20the%20miniature-sized%20Dachshund%20came%20to%20be.

Recommended Reading and Websites

American Kennel Club. (1991). *American kennel club dog care and training.* A Simon & Schuster Macmillan Company.

Anderson, David. (2018). *The complete guide to miniature dachshunds: A step-by-step guide to successfully raising your new miniature dachshund.* CreateSpace Independent Publishing Platform.

Animals Network Team. (n.d.). *Rat terrier.* https://animals.net/rat-terrier/

ASPCA Pet Poison Control. (n.d.). *A vital resource for understanding common pet toxins and how to keep your dachshund safe.* https://www.aspca.org/pet-care/animal-poison-control

Carey, A. (1995). *The dachshund: An owner's guide to a happy healthy pet.* A Simon & Schuster Macmillan Company.

Dachshund Central. (n.d.). *Dachshund Central: A hub for dachshund history, health, and community, featuring articles and owner resources.* https://dachshund-central.com

Dachshund Rescue of North America. (n.d.). Information on adoption, fostering, and breed advocacy. https://drna.org/

Fiedelmeier, L. (1994). *Dachshunds: A complete pet owner's manual.* Barron's Educational Series, Inc.

Kaufmand, G. (2023). *Golden retriever puppy diarrhea: Essential tips for pet parents.* https://www.mygoldenretrieverpuppies.com/blog/golden-retriever-puppy-diarrhea

PetMD. (n.d.). *Resource for pet health information.* https://www.petmd.com

Trupanion Pet Blog. (n.d.). *Offers articles on various aspects of pet care, including health tips specifically for dachshunds.* https://trupanion.com/pet-blog

Important Organizations and Clubs for Dachshund Enthusiasts

Dachshund Club of America (DCA)
dachshundclubofamerica.org
(The National Breed Club for Dachshunds in the United States, offering resources on breed standards, health, events, and responsible breeding practices).

Dachshund Rescue of North America (DRNA)
drna.org
(A nonprofit organization focused on rescuing and rehoming Dachshunds in need. They provide resources for adoption, fostering, and breed advocacy).

American Kennel Club (AKC)
akc.org
(The AKC offers resources on dog care, training, and breed information, including standards for Dachshunds).

Dachshund Club of Canada
dachshundclubofcanada.com
(The official club for dachshund enthusiasts in Canada, providing information on events, breed standards, and health resources).

Dachshund Association of New Zealand
dachshund.org.nz
(Promotes the breed through events, education, and advocacy).

Doxie Nation
doxienation.com